Especially for

_____

From

_____

Date

_____

Compiled and written by Nanette Anderson in association with Snapdragon Group℠, Tulsa, OK

ISBN 978-1-61626-227-3

Published by Barbour Publishing, Inc., P.O. Box 719, Uhrichsville, Ohio 44683, www.barbourbooks.com

Our mission is to publish and distribute inspirational products offering exceptional value and biblical encouragement to the masses.

 Member of the
Evangelical Christian
Publishers Association

Printed in China.

Simple
Entertaining

Tips & Ideas

BARBOUR
PUBLISHING

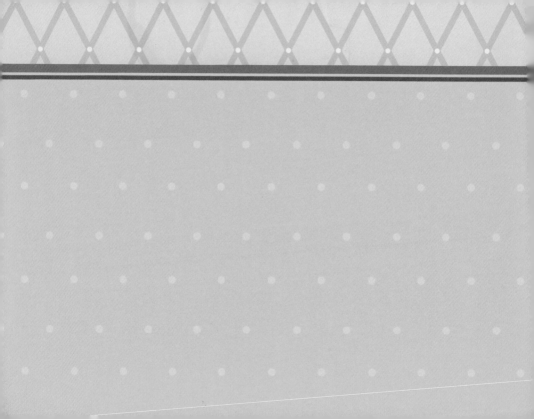

Who practices hospitality
entertains God Himself.

UNKNOWN

The first rule of simple entertaining is to have fun. If you, the host, are enjoying yourself, others will, too. Let your hair down and be real. Be rested and ready, happy to see your friends. Make them know how glad you are to be spending time with them.

. . . .

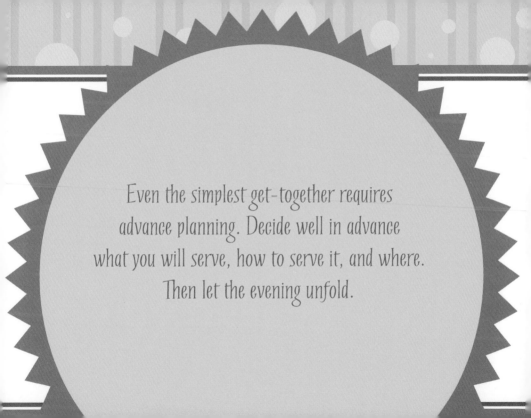

Even the simplest get-together requires advance planning. Decide well in advance what you will serve, how to serve it, and where. Then let the evening unfold.

If you're having a sit-down dinner, set the table the night before. Round up the chairs you need, and decide on a centerpiece. Next day you'll be inspired by the pretty table as you take care of last-minute preparations.

Make sure to have good lighting outside where guests are parking and entering your home. Steps can be tricky in the dark. Make sure your porch has been swept in summer and cleared of snow and ice in winter.

A casual gathering means guests
usually help themselves to food and drink.
Turn your kitchen sink into a built-in
ice chest. Plug the drain and fill with
ice and an assortment of canned
or bottled beverages.

Regardless of how simply you choose to entertain, create some ambience with low-lighting. Lamps and candles do this best. Just make sure you have them safely snuffed out after your guests leave.

Rain or snow keeping you inside? Have an indoor picnic with a sandwich bar and lots of fun extras: chips, pickles, raw veggies, etc. Encourage guests to fix a plate of food and sit anywhere they'd like, even on the floor. Spread out some pretty quilts and throw colorful pillows around the room.

. . . .

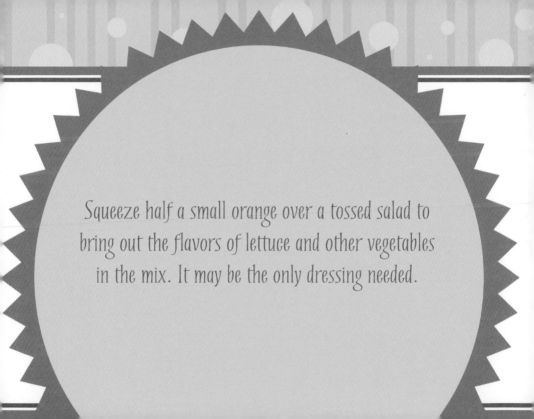

Squeeze half a small orange over a tossed salad to bring out the flavors of lettuce and other vegetables in the mix. It may be the only dressing needed.

Rub a paste of baking soda and a bit of water into charred food burned onto a pan. Let it sit half an hour; then scrub and repeat if necessary.

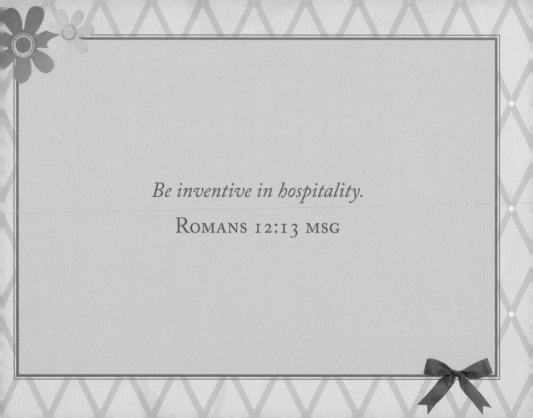

Be inventive in hospitality.

ROMANS 12:13 MSG

Keep track of your costs when entertaining business clients. These can be written off when tax time comes. Remember, this includes your mileage, which can really add up fast.

Keep a record of what you served at each gathering. This way you'll avoid serving the same meal to the same folks too soon. An easy way to do this is to write your meal on a calendar date with the names of guests. Or keep a small journal of dates, guests, and meals served.

If you'd like to have your guests dress casually, tell them so when you issue the invitation. No one likes to appear over (or under) dressed for an occasion, even if it's just a meal in your home. Make them aware if you're planning to serve outdoors so they can bring a sweater or jacket.

. . . .

If guests ask how they can help, give them a simple job to do, like filling water glasses, lighting table candles, cutting a loaf of bread, or tossing a salad. People feel more at home if you let them be involved in some way.

Remember that entertaining and hospitality are not necessarily the same. Entertaining devoid of true hospitality can slide into mere showing off if your guests are made uncomfortable by ostentatious display or overly rigorous manners. Hospitality meets your guests' needs, not your own.

Wear an apron whenever you are in the kitchen after you dress for company. One little splash or mishap can ruin your outfit and your timing if you have to change clothes.

Put long hair up in a bun or ponytail when you're preparing food. You will be much more comfortable and you'll lessen the possibility of a stray strand ending up in your guests' food.

Never apologize if you think your blue ribbon cake
or famous apple pie is not up to your standards.
It forces uncomfortable flattery from your guests.
They will not care if you added a bit too much
sugar or if your crust is not as flaky as usual.

Schedule time to turn on the music, light the candles, and relax before your guests arrive. Take off your apron, put your feet up, and take in the pretty table and your clean, comfortable room. Enjoy the aromas coming from the kitchen.

. . . .

It is not the quantity of the meat, but the cheerfulness of the guests that makes the feast.

LORD CLARENDON

Some of your guests will bring a hostess gift.
Accept it graciously and with thanks, even if the
gift is something you cannot use. You can always
give it away later to someone who will appreciate it.

When you cook, plan to make more than you will serve. Leftovers are great and will save time during the coming week. Pull out leftover roasts for an impromptu sandwich lunch with a neighbor, or take an easy-heat meal to the shut-in down the block.

When planning a dinner party, set up your coffee and tea service ahead of time. Get out the service pieces you'll need for sugar and cream, and have dessert dishes and extra utensils ready to go on when dinnerware is cleared.

An easy way to make a dinner more festive is to serve drinks in fancy glasses. The fancier, the better. Pinkies up!

The busiest day ahead of any entertaining is not the day of, but the day before! Do all your cleaning and shopping one or two days out, and prepare anything you can make ahead the day before. Keep your schedule clear of all but last-minute projects on the day of your party.

. . . .

If you've been noticing that your kitchen linens or rugs are looking a little overworked and shabby, replace them before a party. These are things guests tend to notice and appreciate, and they give your kitchen an immediate face-lift.

A good time to move your guests into another room for conversation and a change of position is before that second round of coffee. Encourage them to bring along their coffee or tea, and freshen drinks once everyone is settled.

Stick to tried-and-true recipes when entertaining. Your guests are not guinea pigs! Making a dish for the first time creates tension for you, and with the other normal stresses of entertaining, you don't need to worry about how a first attempt will come out.

Nothing grates on guests' nerves like loud, distracting music. Unless you are choosing a particular type of music for a particular type of party, rely on soft, relaxing instrumentals playing throughout the evening, and keep the volume low.

Be hospitable to one another
without grumbling.

1 PETER 4:9 NKJV

Avoid overwhelming your dinner guests with huge portions.
Start with a small amount and always offer seconds.

. . . .

Keep candle lighters in a convenient spot. Make sure ahead of time that they are working properly. If not, you run the risk of having to dig through cluttered drawers for a lighter or matches with guests looking on or waiting at the table.

Fresh flowers are a huge enhancement to any dinner table or serving buffet. They need not be expensive. A supermarket bouquet costs only a few dollars and can be cut down or rearranged to fit your table setting.

Keep appetizers for your dinner party light. You don't want to spoil your guests' appetites before the main event! Offer rice crackers and small slices of cheese. Or serve shrimp cocktail. One or two of these will leave plenty of room for dinner.

Avoid rushing your guests to the dinner table. Let your dinner finish cooking or keep it warm while you relax over drinks and appetizers with your guests. This puts the focus on them rather than the meal. When conversation is flowing, slip out to get ready to serve and only then invite everyone into the dining room.

Think ahead about the number of guests, seating, meal plan, table setting, and grocery shopping. Walk mentally through the evening, making lists and notes for everything you want to do. You will inevitably encounter last-minute surprises, but you will handle them easily if you are well prepared.

If your tap water smells or tastes unusual, buy a couple gallons of filtered drinking water to serve your guests. Keep a pitcher of it on the table throughout the meal and dessert.

. . . .

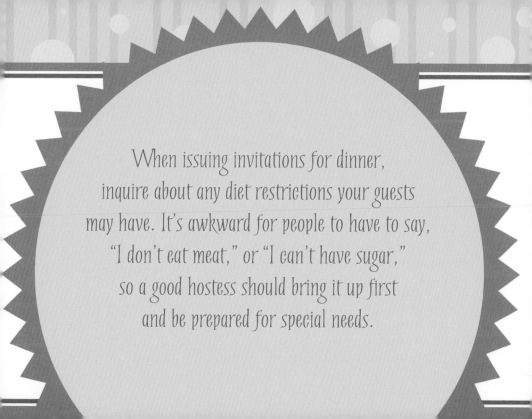

When issuing invitations for dinner, inquire about any diet restrictions your guests may have. It's awkward for people to have to say, "I don't eat meat," or "I can't have sugar," so a good hostess should bring it up first and be prepared for special needs.

Is one person dominating the conversation? Has talk turned to gossip or negative and unappetizing topics? Turning the focus requires a hostess's deft handling and should be invisible. Ask a quiet guest a question in another direction; move the group to another room; offer to freshen drinks. Have a few positive topics to seamlessly redirect the conversation.

Let not the emphasis of hospitality lie in bed and board; but let truth and love and honor and courtesy flow in all thy deeds.

RALPH WALDO EMERSON

If you find that entertaining is something you really enjoy, take stock of your dinnerware and serving pieces. Start collecting pieces you need and want. Budget a little money each month to invest in that casserole dish, soup tureen, meat platter, or serving bowl set. Buy matching or interchangeable pieces. If you replace china, consider all white; it goes with anything.

Keep some good quality snacks on hand to serve when guests drop in unexpectedly. Rolled cookies are sold in airtight tins and keep well in the pantry. Support the Girl Scouts and keep a couple boxes of their cookies on the shelf. Shortbread and Thin Mints are always favorites.

If your wax candles melt onto the tablecloth, invert and stretch the affected fabric over a bowl and pour boiling water onto it until the wax melts and drips away.

· ·

Simple entertaining may include paper plates and cups now and again when big groups are expected and the menu is very simple and light. Just make sure you buy a sturdy brand or double-plate the cheaper kind.

If you get caught with time for only one quick house cleanup before last-minute company, make it dusting. Then, if time allows, use a broom on the kitchen floor and put out a clean hand towel in the guest bath.

Learn to make jam. It sounds hard, but it really isn't, and nothing pleases guests like being offered homemade jam.

Many guests enjoy contributing a dish to dinner, so if they ask, say yes. It makes them feel loved and accepted even before their feet cross your threshold.

Learn to make soups. They can be fast to whip up at the last minute, and they're cheap and almost universally loved.

Banana splits are a fun dessert. For maximum fun, put all the fixin's out on the kitchen counter or island and invite guests to create their own.

. . . .

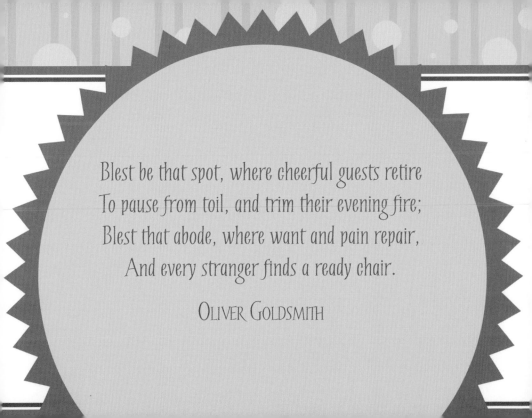

Blest be that spot, where cheerful guests retire
To pause from toil, and trim their evening fire;
Blest that abode, where want and pain repair,
And every stranger finds a ready chair.

Oliver Goldsmith

Sometimes your guests will be overnighters.
Check the bath they will use and make sure there
is a bar of soap in the shower, plenty of towels,
and a small basket of essentials for their use.
Restock toilet paper and give all surfaces a
last-minute shine with glass cleaner.

Simple entertaining often means buffet-line serving. Set the table with napkins and utensils only. Stack plates and drinking glasses near food and drinks for self-service. If the in and out of a large group at the table is too congested or disruptive, pass dishes around in family style. Be sure to space little children between helpful adults.

Keep water flowing. A good hostess keeps her eye on water glasses and fills them when they get low. A bowl of ice set out on the table is a good idea as well.

Even the most extravagant meal can be simply presented if well planned. Try to avoid jumping up several times as the meal gets underway; make sure spoons are in all the serving dishes, candles are lit. Don't forget salt and pepper, butter, etc.

*If the meal you are planning is heavy,
make dessert very light, and vice versa.*

. . . .

Use your fireplace when guests come over.
It makes a warm, instant welcome
and a feeling of being at home.

Candles on the table are wonderful in the evening,
even if a meal as simple as chili and
cornbread is being served.

Have a few packages of high-quality embossed napkins on hand for those occasions when you don't need or want to use cloth.

Put pets in the garage or another closed room when guests are expected. As much as you enjoy the company of your furry friends, your visitors may be annoyed by the dog foraging under the table or a cat that wants to cuddle. The same goes for the loud bird in the living room that you have learned to tune out.

Serve wholeheartedly, as if you were serving the Lord, not men, because you know that the Lord will reward everyone for whatever good he does.

EPHESIANS 6:7–8

Inexpensive glass cups and small glass plates can come in handy in almost any serving situation—from bread and salad to dessert; and because they're clear, they go with any china pattern. They can be found in discount stores or at a big box outlet.

. . . .

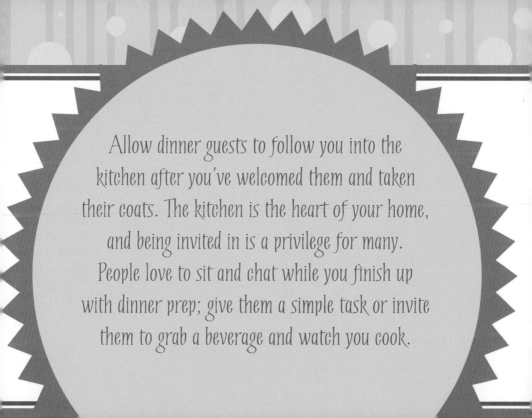

Allow dinner guests to follow you into the kitchen after you've welcomed them and taken their coats. The kitchen is the heart of your home, and being invited in is a privilege for many. People love to sit and chat while you finish up with dinner prep; give them a simple task or invite them to grab a beverage and watch you cook.

How's the temperature in your home?
If you regularly keep it unusually cold or warm,
you may need to bring temperatures up or
down accordingly for your guests. If they are
uncomfortable, that is what they will remember
about their evening in your home. Regardless
of the weather, open the house for a few minutes
and air it out before guests arrive.

Always buy unscented candles. The perfumed types can be overpowering and can even distaste your meal. The wonderful smells of your cooking will be the best aroma for your guests.

Plan a simple protein-rich breakfast for overnight guests in your home. Also have cereal available and toaster out for those who just want a piece of toast to start the day.

Always wash and dry new stiff, scratchy sheets and towels at least three times before using them for sleepover company. This makes them soft and absorbent.

Learn to use your slow cooker, especially if you work outside the home. There is no end to the wonderful meals that can be cooking during the day while you're away.

. . . .

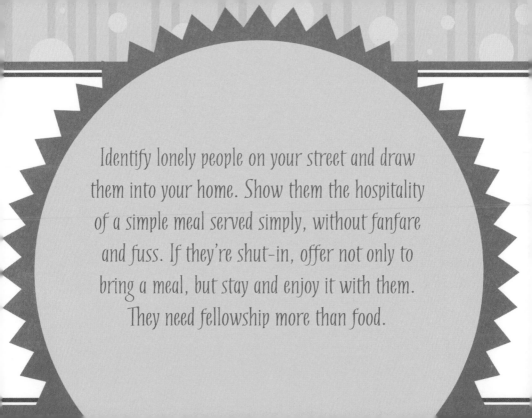

Identify lonely people on your street and draw them into your home. Show them the hospitality of a simple meal served simply, without fanfare and fuss. If they're shut-in, offer not only to bring a meal, but stay and enjoy it with them. They need fellowship more than food.

When you bake muffins, make extra and drop them off with the church secretary for your pastor and his family. This is a gift of love that speaks volumes.

There is an emanation from the heart in
genuine hospitality which cannot be described,
but is immediately felt and puts the
stranger at once at his ease.

WASHINGTON IRVING

When inviting in a couple who are on a tight budget, offer to provide your teenager for free babysitting so they can come as a twosome and have a night out alone. If you have no willing teen to ask, offer to pay and let your guests choose their own sitter.

De-clutter your house for company. Whether they come for a meal or for an extended stay, remove piles of magazines, bills, work projects, and stray toys. Clear serving areas and end tables enough to allow a dessert dish or cup and saucer to be placed there uncrowded.

When entertaining, offer real cream, sugar, and butter. You may want to have the substitutes for these on hand, but present dinner guests with the real thing first.

. . . .

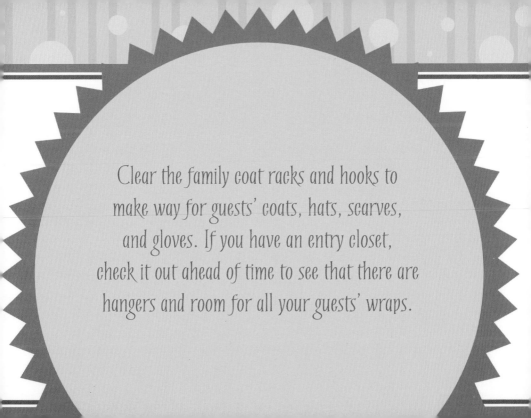

Clear the family coat racks and hooks to make way for guests' coats, hats, scarves, and gloves. If you have an entry closet, check it out ahead of time to see that there are hangers and room for all your guests' wraps.

Other than your dining room table all set
for company, nothing speaks louder than the guest
bath. Be sure it is scrubbed and polished from top
to bottom and smells wonderful. A small nightlight
or a very lightly scented candle has a nice effect.

You may be used to seeing that tired old rug or frayed towel in the guest bath, but it is a poor impression on your guests. Invest in fresh, new linens if your old ones are faded and worn.

Keep club soda on hand to clean up spills on carpet and clothing. Immediately pour on club soda and blot with a clean rag until the stain is removed.

If you have tablecloths, use them.
They soften words and the clatter of
dinner and add richness to your china.

Invest in pretty placemats as an occasional alternative to a tablecloth. Choose patterns that are not too loud, and avoid rigid styles that lead to upsets or scratch your table's wood.

. . . .

It is an excellent circumstance that hospitality
grows best where it is most needed.

HUGH MILLER

Turn off the TV! Turn off the radio!
Turn off the phone, your cell, and your pager
during mealtimes. Even if you are only eating with
family, they will appreciate the value you place on
uninterrupted conversation, and the rest of the
world can wait thirty minutes while you dine!

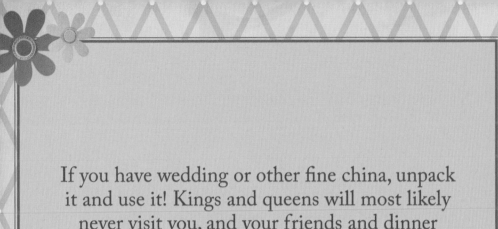

If you have wedding or other fine china, unpack it and use it! Kings and queens will most likely never visit you, and your friends and dinner guests will feel like royalty eating off it.

Plan meals that don't require both you and your spouse to be hovering over the stove or grill together. One of you needs to focus exclusively on entertaining guests while the other sees to finishing up in the kitchen and serving.

There are going to be those occasions when you've done everything right, but guests don't click and conversation stalls. Have some topics ready, or ask questions that will spark lively discussion. Ask where your guests grew up. Or ask about family. . . people love to talk about their children.

Keep a notebook with your cookbooks and record meals that worked particularly well and combinations of foods that complemented each other. Write in everything from appetizers through dessert, even table settings and centerpieces you want to remember to use again.

. . . .

Place a handwritten welcome to guests on a small kitchen island chalkboard. There are entertainment pieces available for this purpose in houseware sections of department stores: a pig in a chef hat holding a chalkboard; a jolly Italian baker riding his bike; a chef wearing a message board saying, WELCOME, DENNIS AND BECKY.

Messy appetizers are okay if you also provide small plates and napkins. Avoid your guests' embarrassment over cocktail sauce or cheese dip dribbling onto furniture or carpets.

Revive the old-fashioned potluck. Assign main dish, salad, bread, and dessert, and let your guests pull out the stops or make something simple if they choose. Set up your table or buffet area and let the fun begin!

Issue a meal invitation to a family with whom you worship regularly, or to a family or individual who has been visiting your church lately. Call early Sunday morning and ask them to come for lunch after church. Do the cooking on Saturday, and keep it simple. Save the big fried chicken and mashed potatoes feast for another time and make this get-together about friends and fellowship with an impromptu feel.

If anyone serves, he should do it with the strength God provides, so that in all things God may be praised through Jesus Christ.

1 PETER 4:11

Invest in a well-fitted dining table pad and stop worrying about water or heat damage to your fine wood table. This allows you to dispense with trivets and wads of kitchen towels under casseroles and sweating glassware.

. . . .

Whatever type of get-together you have planned, try to wind up the activities by 9 p.m., so guests will feel free to leave without guilt that they have interrupted your plans.

Serving the main dish from a hot, heavy casserole dish? Place it near your seat and invite guests to pass their plates to you for service.

Start a collection of eclectic china place settings. The effect is charming when each guest is eating from a totally unique pattern, and prompts conversation about how you acquired each setting from travels, estate sales, garage sales, etc. Use white or solid linens to draw the look together.

When a guest compliments an item of décor in your home, resist the temptation to tell them where you bought it and how much it cost. Even if it was an incredible bargain, just say "thank you" and leave it at that. This applies to the outfit and jewelry you're wearing, as well!

Even if you have a rule in your family about removing shoes when you enter the house, don't require it of your guests. Many people need their shoes on for walking ease or simply feel uncomfortable without them.

Being prepared for company in advance includes your personal preparation as well. Be dressed and ready thirty minutes ahead of guests' arrival and prop your feet up for a few minutes. Some guests do arrive early, and you don't want to be drying your hair when the doorbell rings!

. . . .

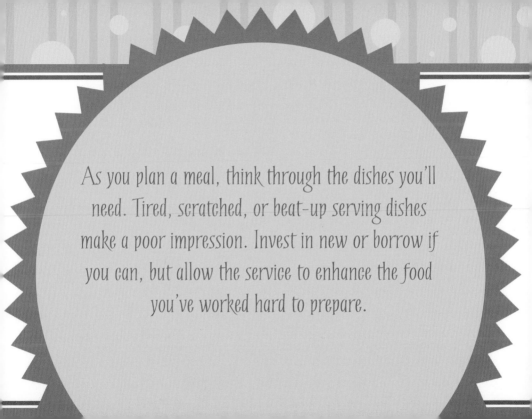

As you plan a meal, think through the dishes you'll need. Tired, scratched, or beat-up serving dishes make a poor impression. Invest in new or borrow if you can, but allow the service to enhance the food you've worked hard to prepare.

Plan a soup or chili cook-off in your home with a few good friends. They will be providing an abundant main course while you see to sides, beverages, and dessert.

The ultimate aim of civility and good manners is to please: to please one's guest or to please one's host. To this end one uses the rules laid down by tradition: of welcome, generosity, affability, cheerfulness, and consideration for others.

CLAUDIA RODEN

Place paper-thin slices of lemon in
glasses of water as you fill them
ahead of sitting down to eat.

Chocolate chip cookies are always. . .yes, always a winner! You can never go wrong with them as long as they're homemade and same-day fresh!

If the entertainment you're planning includes games, say so in the invitation. People either love them or hate them. Allow those who find board games, charades, or cards excruciating to politely bow out right off the bat.

. . . .

Take your hospitality to the streets. Make jam or bread or cookies and deliver them to the near neighbors who have been difficult to meet in other ways. Introduce yourself and step in for a few minutes if you're asked. As you leave, encourage them to feel free to drop in on you at home.

When whole families are coming over, have an area away from adults where children can go to be noisy. Provide toys, games, or put on a movie or video game for them. Sometimes it is perfectly acceptable to feed the kids first and let them go play elsewhere while the adults eat and visit.

Keep your napkins, tablecloths, and napkin rings in a convenient place. Wash and iron items promptly after your party and put them away for the next use. This is a time-consuming task that should be done way ahead of time, so it doesn't throw your timing off the day of the event.

Check out your table before guests arrive.
Be sure you have salt and pepper, butter,
serving spoons, and a pitcher of water—
so you're not popping up every few minutes
once the meal is under way.

When entertaining overnight guests, prepare messy breakfast meats in advance. Frying and cleanup can be done days ahead, meat stored in the refrigerator and popped into the microwave for a minute to reheat and crisp up.

Store bags of pre-cut veggies in your freezer. Onions, peppers, and celery will be readily available for quick meal preparation. Keep a good-quality ice cream on hand as well. It's a delicious ready-made dessert when you don't have time to bake something fresh.

. . . .

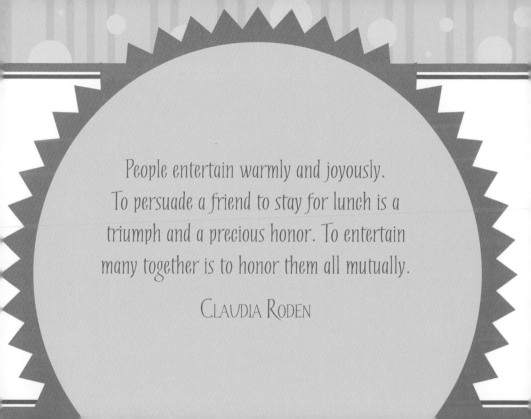

People entertain warmly and joyously.
To persuade a friend to stay for lunch is a
triumph and a precious honor. To entertain
many together is to honor them all mutually.

CLAUDIA RODEN

Put a tray of tortilla chips in a hot oven for just a few minutes. They will crisp up nicely, and your guests will love them warm.

A variety of short, fat, skinny, and uniquely colored candles makes a pretty glow for entertaining at the table. Set three or four candles on a small plate together. Arrange two plates and place them on either side of a simple vase of flowers.

Keep centerpieces low so that guests can talk over, not through, them. A too-big flower arrangement separates diners and interrupts conversation.

Mark a special occasion by sending your guests home with a favor. Small jars of homemade jam or tiny loaves of bread are always appreciated.

Around the holidays, decorate with evergreen boughs you trimmed from your Christmas tree before you put it up. After you trim them off, just store them on the back porch until you're ready for them. Pine is beautiful and fresh and looks elegant when placed around a candle's soft glow on the table or mantel.

. . . .

For a change of pace, move hors d'oeuvres to the family or living room to serve. Bring in the drinks, too, and provide napkins and small plates.

If you have an herb garden, bring in sprigs of rosemary and include them on your table for fragrance. Place them in a vase and pass them out to guests to refresh hands after the meal.

Serving shellfish, ribs, or fried chicken can be messy even with a large napkin. Delight your guests with warm, moist towels. Buy new white washcloths, roll them up, wet them, and pop them in the microwave for a minute. Serve them from a pretty tray after dinner and before dessert.

Save leftover or stale dinner bread and freeze it. Use it for french toast or to make into croutons for salad another day.

Give freely and spontaneously. Don't have a stingy heart.
The way you handle matters like this triggers GOD,
your God's, blessing in everything you do,
all your work and ventures.

DEUTERONOMY 15:10 MSG

Go outside the side-dish box. Serve sweet potatoes instead of white; try coleslaw in place of a regular dinner salad. Or serve your main dish with polenta, easy to make and readily available in supermarkets.

. . . .

Learn how to make a really good spaghetti sauce from scratch. Make it in large batches and freeze meal-size containers for a super quick and hearty meal. Your friends will think you slaved over the stove all day!

Keep a pretty box of facial tissues available
for guests in every room in which you entertain.
Don't make them run to the bathroom or
grab a napkin when they sneeze!

Drape pretty, soft throws over sofas and armchairs. Guests love pulling them into their laps if they get chilly.

Throw a "grill party." Invite guests to bring whatever meat they want to grill, and you fix sides, bread, and dessert. This is a hearty and economical way to give people just the meal they like. It also brings a lot of variety and fun to the evening.

Freshen up your front porch area with a pot of supermarket petunias or pansies when you're inviting friends over. If the weather is too cold, make a door wreath with real branches or boughs to improve that first impression.

Keep a fresh assortment of good quality teabags in a pretty wooden box or ornate bowl to serve guests who prefer tea. Be sure to include some herbal or decaffeinated varieties.

. . . .

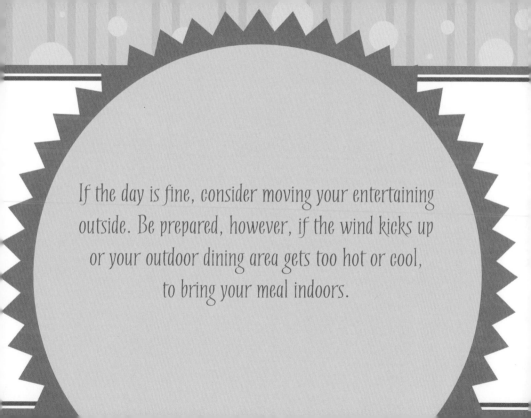

If the day is fine, consider moving your entertaining outside. Be prepared, however, if the wind kicks up or your outdoor dining area gets too hot or cool, to bring your meal indoors.

Have a game party with kids and parents.
Set up card tables and have games set up
and ready to go. Place an adult or two at
each table and provide bowls of homemade
party mix, popcorn, nuts, pretzels, and candy.
Serve drinks in the can for stability.

In hospitality the chief thing is goodwill.

GREEK PROVERB

Keep a good-sized bowl near you when you're preparing food or baking. Toss anything into it that you want to throw away—eggshells, butter wrappers, refuse from vegetable or meat trimming, etc. One trip to the trash can, and you're done!

Buy plastic bins that will slide under your island or onto a cabinet or pantry shelf. Keep in it all the baking supplies you regularly use. When you're ready to whip up a cake or some cookies, just pull out your baking bin and you have everything you need ready to go.

When preparing a meal, have a large bowl or one side of your sink full of hot, soapy water. Toss in anything you're finished with to soak, or quickly wash things you need to reuse. When it's time to load the dishwasher, your prep dishes will be already rinsed for easy clean-up.

. . . .

E-vites are fine for simple entertaining occasions, but use the telephone if you want to issue a last-minute invitation.

Use a thermal coffee carafe or two to serve gravy
at large dinners like Thanksgiving or Christmas.
Gravy never gets to people fast enough when so
many dishes are making their way around.
The carafe holds a lot of gravy and keeps
it good and hot at the table.

Nothing is so welcoming as the sight of you standing out on your porch when first-time guests come to your home. They will be straining to see house numbers and identify landmarks you've given them, but seeing you smiling and waving them in is a wonderful welcome.

Save bones from hams, steaks, or roasts along with the bits of meat left clinging to them. Wrap them and keep them handy in the freezer to boil up with broth for soups. If you accumulate too many, ask your neighbor if you can give them for a treat to his dog!

Organize your spice racks or rounds alphabetically to easily locate the flavoring you need. Or organize spices in groups that you commonly use for particular dishes.

Pre-treat and put stained tablecloths and napkins into a cold-water soak in your washing machine as soon as possible after guests leave. Let them soak overnight, then drain and run them through a wash cycle.

. . . .

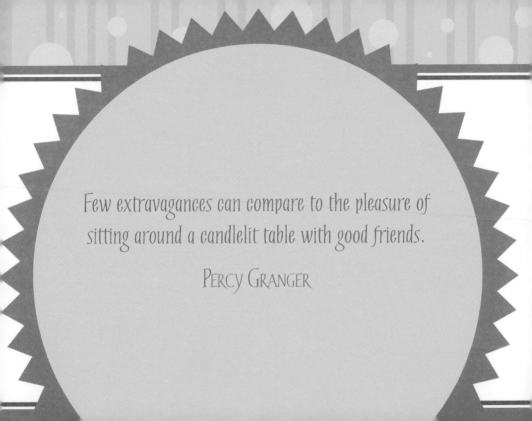

Few extravagances can compare to the pleasure of sitting around a candlelit table with good friends.

PERCY GRANGER

Don't hesitate to rearrange furniture a bit when having guests in. Try to create a comfortable setting for easy conversation. Bring in an extra easy chair and ottoman from another room, and clear end and coffee tables for serving dessert or setting drinks on.

Candle wax spilled on carpet can be removed by letting it dry and harden, then covering with a lightweight cloth. Press the cloth with a very hot iron to melt the wax, and let it absorb into the cloth. Keep moving the cloth to a clean patch for fresh absorption and to keep from sending absorbed wax back into your rug.

Use three-way bulbs in the lamps in your conversation area. Use the lowest setting when relaxing with guests.

If you're entertaining in winter, reserve space in your crowded refrigerator by placing drinks in a snowbank outside or setting them on the step just outside your kitchen door until you're ready to serve them.

If you live in a warm climate year-round, use your camp cooler.

Napkin rings add flair to your dinner table setting, and with a little creativity you can make your own. Tie pretty ribbon around napkins, twine and tie some raffia, or choose floral sprays attached to covered floral wire and simply curl around napkins. Use a pinecone for holding a place card, or hot glue it to raffia in a ring for napkins.

. . . .

Keep paper doilies in various sizes on hand.
They dress up plates in a big way
for dessert presentation.

Buy your meat at Costco or Sam's Club. The cuts are far superior and every bit as economical as the supermarket variety. Invest in whole loins of meat and cut them yourself into steaks the size you desire. Unless bones are involved, a few simple knife strokes at home saves you up to two dollars per pound that the butcher charges for ready-cut meat.

Unless you simply love to bake bread, try out one of the wonderful hot loaves available from the supermarket. Higher quality is found in specialty loaves, also available at the store. Or drop by a bakery for a delicious ready-baked loaf, and use the time you save for a bubble bath before company arrives.

Resist the temptation to correct your spouse unnecessarily when you entertain as a couple. Your guests don't care if the situation he is describing was Tuesday or Wednesday. They are hopefully listening to an entertaining story and won't know the difference in meaningless details. Don't discomfort them by interrupting.

A generous man will prosper;
he who refreshes others
will himself be refreshed.

PROVERBS 11:25

Keep a couple half gallons of good ice cream in your freezer for a fast treat for unexpected guests or for an easy dessert when you're running short on time.

. . . .

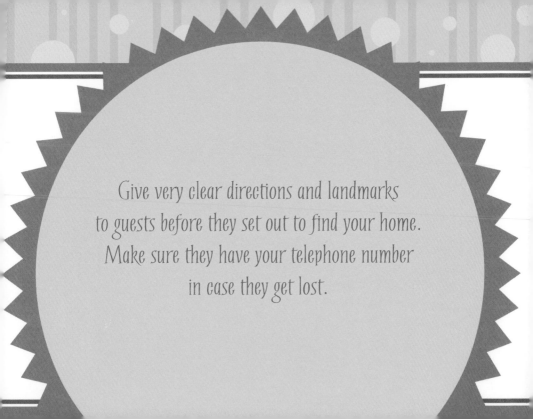

Give very clear directions and landmarks
to guests before they set out to find your home.
Make sure they have your telephone number
in case they get lost.

Remember, it is not so much what you serve
to dinner guests or what you serve it on—
what people really love is that you cared
enough to invite them over.

Once in a while you will have a guest who just insists on helping you clean up. If you absolutely want to avoid this, say, "Let's just stack our plates in the kitchen. I'll get to it later. Right now I just want to visit with *you*." This way, the guest feels she's helped, and then feels free to move to the living room and chat.

If you find yourself in a pinch for time, use high-quality, canned crescent rolls. Hot out of the oven and served with jam and butter, they are surefire winners!

Use a thermal pump coffee pot for large gatherings. While you serve from it, another pot of coffee can be brewing.

Entertaining need not always involve dinner.
Invite friends over for dessert or a light snack
after choir practice or the school play.

. . . .

Shop secondhand and thrift stores for the old-fashioned glass plate/cup combos. They are in vogue again and will begin to be hard to find. They come in quite handy for serving drinks and appetizers or dessert and coffee.

Pull your punch bowl off the shelf and use it!
Nothing creates instant flair like a pretty bowl of
refreshing punch surrounded by glass party cups.
Allow guests to serve themselves.

May your home always be too small
to hold all of your friends.

UNKNOWN

Save fine china table settings for adult-only occasions. Kids are clumsy by nature and their parents will have a very uptight meal if too many precious breakables are in their children's path.

When a prospective guest—one you know is an excellent baker—asks to bring something, let her make bread or dessert. It will free you to concentrate on other things you do very well.

Make sure your table linens are freshly washed and ironed.
A beautiful table setting with candles, flowers,
and fine china will be spoiled by stained napkins
or a wrinkled tablecloth.

. . . .

Make an ice ring of fruit and juices if you plan to use a punch bowl. They take a long time to freeze, so do it a few days in advance. If your fruit is not citrus, stir in a few teaspoons of lemon juice before freezing to keep fruit from browning. As the ring melts in the punch, it freshens it. Add a little more ginger ale each hour.

Check your ice maker and make sure it is working well before a function where you will need lots of ice. You won't want your husband running out to the 7-11 just as guests are arriving!

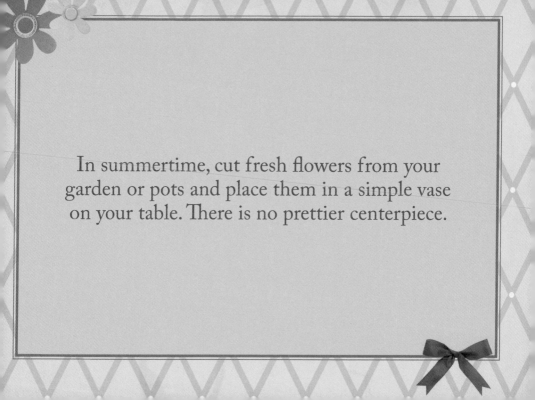

In summertime, cut fresh flowers from your garden or pots and place them in a simple vase on your table. There is no prettier centerpiece.

Just before offering thanks ahead of the meal, make eye contact with each of your guests and thank them for coming to your table. Then let the man of the house lead in saying grace.

If you have borrowed special meal service items from friends, wash and pack them carefully afterward and return them within a day or two of your event; your friends will be happy to lend them again the next time you ask.

Use your slow cooker for keeping dips and hot drinks like wassail at a constant temperature for serving. Check out the smaller ones stores now carry. They're cute and very handy.

. . . .

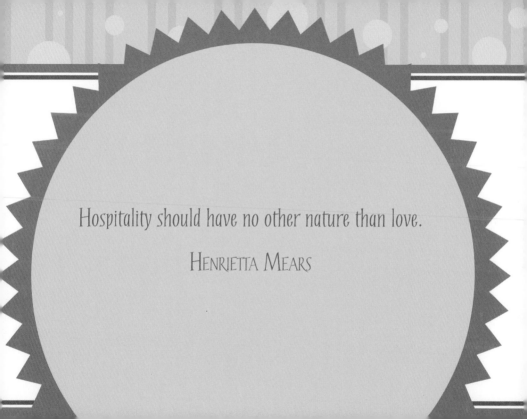

Hospitality should have no other nature than love.

HENRIETTA MEARS

Try to keep a good-quality beef summer sausage
and some good cheese in your refrigerator.
They make a quick last-minute appetizer.

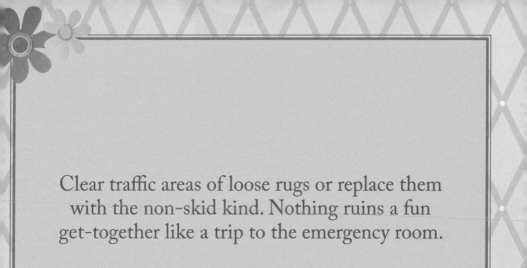

Clear traffic areas of loose rugs or replace them with the non-skid kind. Nothing ruins a fun get-together like a trip to the emergency room.

If you are burning your fireplace as you entertain, crack a window somewhere. Gas log and wood fires use up the oxygen in your room over several hours and can make it hard to breathe and stay awake.

Stow personal business papers, bills, notes, and private information from areas your guests will have access to.

Shop and stockpile discounted or past-season tableware and paper products like cocktail napkins, paper plates, and towels. At full price these are budget busters!

. . . .

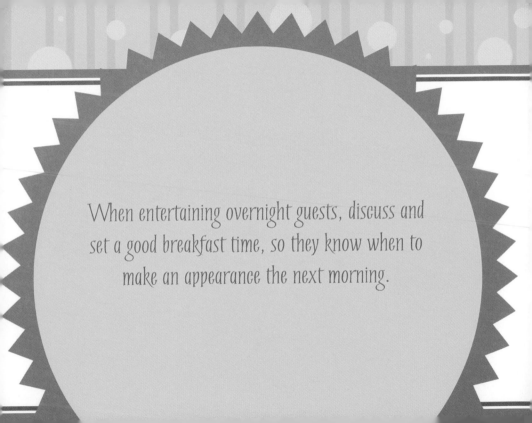

When entertaining overnight guests, discuss and set a good breakfast time, so they know when to make an appearance the next morning.

When families with toddlers visit, remove and put up anything you couldn't endure being damaged. Even the best-behaved kids will inadvertently bump into things. So do yourself and your guests a favor and put breakables away before they arrive.

When invited to someone's home for the first time, take a hostess gift. It need not be expensive or extravagant. Something homemade is best, like jam or a jar of some other home-canned goods. Boxed chocolates, pretty note cards, or a small potted plant are also excellent choices.

Look with a critical eye at the carpets in your home. Are they looking soiled and traffic worn? Have them professionally cleaned at least once a year to keep them in good shape and presentable when you entertain.

The ornaments of your house are
the guests who frequent it.

UNKNOWN

Kids like to entertain, too, and this is an opportunity for you to teach them valuable hospitality skills. Help them plan a party or gathering of friends. Offer to help with the food, game, or movie ideas, and help them think through and pre-plan the entire event. They will appreciate how much work goes into doing it right.

. . . .

If your pet usually eats and drinks in your kitchen, remove food and water bowls before the arrival of dinner guests, some of whom find that sort of thing unsavory.

Modern sofas and armchairs are usually too crowded up with decorative pillows for comfortable guest seating. Remove at least half beforehand, or place them on the floor next to the couch, so your guest won't feel like she is un-decorating your living room to find a seat.

If you love cooking with fresh herbs, start a tiny windowsill herb garden. Supermarkets regularly sell small, inexpensive pots of mint, oregano, basil, and other popular spice herbs. Even in the middle of winter, you will be able to pinch a fresh leaf whenever you need it.

Women love a tea party. Learn to brew loose tea and serve it with fresh-baked scones or baking powder biscuits and some homemade strawberry jam. Offer rich whipped cream, and use your best china cups and saucers, dessert plates, and pretty cloth napkins.

Begin a blog for posting your favorite recipes and entertaining tips. You will be amazed at how much useful information will come to you in return! Start small and let your entertaining expertise grow over time. It isn't as hard as it seems. Practice makes perfect. Blessings!